Inward Bloom: Whispers of Growth, Love, & Renewal

Michala Payne

BookLeaf Publishing

India | USA | UK

Presentation by *BookLeaf Publishing*

Web: www.bookleafpub.com

E-mail: info@bookleafpub.com

ISBN: 9789358317275

First edition 2024

*This collection is dedicated to my
great-grandmother, Queen Elizabeth Smith, and
my husband, George Payne Jr.*

Whispers of a Wilted Rose

Can you hear her?
That deafening fear
Any time I stand still she whispers in my ear,
"Life is passing you by, and Oh! You're
forgetting to breathe.
The earth is doing circles while you're down
here on your knees"
Then I catch my breath and I focus in
Because it'll be hell or high water before she
wins
But again it happens, and I'm at a loss
Look, it's harder than you think showing her
who's the boss
It's like a constant battle between left and right
It's like never knowing who's up next to fight
It's like being too happy or being too sad
It's constantly hearing "oh, it's not that bad"
It's not knowing when it's too much or when it's
not enough
It's constantly wondering when she's going to
give up
She's silent but loud, and she creeps up quick
Please tell me…can you hear her? Or am I really
losing it?

Vanilla Orchids

On a Sunday afternoon lost in conversation
television runnin', fan buzzin', heat strokin'
Jimmy Swaggart hymnals
It's never been louder, and I sense I hear
someone,
Calling me.
Fragrant aromas of young memories I can't
recall
Sitting beside a wall of a stained glass window
Who's calling me?
Verbal symphonies of discord, lost between
chords
of dissonance
Hysterical laughter of past times trying to pass
time,
But time should've been frozen
Frozen as we wanted to be on a hot summer's
day
But we couldn't because of the Queen
Sitting high on her throne making the house a
home
Frozen like our hearts were on that dreaded day
in May
Though our hearts vetted and etched with the
Queen's decree

Everything seemed to fade into on solid memory
Vanilla, pure, sweet
Calling me
To be lost in conversation on a Sunday
afternoon.

Wilting Lillies

Girl, you were my A1 since day 1, how it work
like that?
Whatever happened to make this day
come...y'know it hurts thinking back
but on the real the biggest deal to me
is how we had conjured up all these fantasies
of places we would see, who we wanted to be
and now it's just a memory
you were the unspoken godmother to my unborn
child
thoughts and dreams of how our kids would run
wild
for miles and miles in that countryside field
because we knew how it'd feel
but now the feeling is stale
it's like we went through hell with hail
thinking it wouldn't evaporate, much like this
friendship
and nah girl, it's not hate just fate
that brought us here
we had been down for many years, cried many
tears, even made up cheers
but cheers to the life we have created separately
sometimes friendships just aren't meant to be

and it's bittersweet watching them wilt into
memory

African Violets

Nestled in a pot so deep, ever bloomin'
lost in the hues of his petals
swoonin'
petals so silky caressin' every
inch of my garden
fallin'
rich, dark soil breathin' life
to the roots being intertwined
devoted to
lines upon lines of past times
rollin' into one beautiful oasis
it don't make no sense
how I'm feelin'
it's different
all I can say is an African Violet bloomin' did it
so fragile but strong
so gentle, I long
I long for the times I can embrace his scent
like I said, it just don't make no sense
whipped

Weeds

Sometimes there for good
mostly looked as bad
growin' high to the sky
gravity bring me back

full to the brim
over my limit
lost between what is
and what isn't

"makin my --- itch"
that's what my momma would say
subversion, diverging
sometimes stuff gets in the way

praying for a way out
when He already gave me a way in
mostly looked as bad
always good in the end

Overgrown Daffodils

Like a daffodil at first sight
small
but just enough to cause a scene
what does the thought of being "grown" really
mean?

Is it the freedom adulthood brings
or in the way accountability clings?
Is it the essence of searching the unknown
but realizing you never left home?

Is it rose-colored glasses we're given at birth
that provides the delusion of being grown's
worth?
Is it woven in the tapestries of life's dwindling
time
or is it lost between the rhythms of an innocent
child's mind?

Wherever it maybe, wherever it is found
I hope it finds me growing from the underground
I want to be rooted
I want to be grown that's true
but its also something
I wish I never knew

Evening Primrose

What a time to be alive
though my social battery is dead
I could have really went
to bed an hour ago
I pushed forward instead

Room full of scents, conversations I rather not
remember
cause whew! If some of the talk didn't burn
through me like hot embers
why she do that? and who said what?
that's probably why my battery is drained
Almost had to ---- somebody up

Night receding now, time has
surely passed
one more week and we
back at it, alas!

First Bloom

Daybreak and I'm still tired
Daybreak and I'm thinking about what it's like
to be fired

Daybreak and I'm on the way up the stairs
Daybreak and I'm wondering what's up with my
hair

Daybreak and I'm late but that's not new
Daybreak and I'm on the way to the trap house
(My bad, I mean the school.)

Daybreak and I hear sailors in the hall cussing
Daybreak and all you hear is yelling and fussing

Midday and I'm tryna remember the last time I
taught
Midday and that's the second time this week my
student done got caught

Midday and I've repeated myself fiftyleven
times
Midday and I'm tired of all the whines

Midday and I'm tired again
Midday and I can't wait for the day to end

Poison Ivy

Crawlin' and creepin'
Layin' roots on things you shouldn't
Honey, you poison and you knew it
Disgusted, disappointed, disowned
Let you in my home
And you ruined it
Sneakin' and slidin' in places
Not meant for you
And you brought it to plant in my garden too!
How dare you?
Toxic.
Make me sick.

Frostbitten Cranberries

If I fixate on a moment
It becomes cemented in my memory
Forever putting fear in me giving me anxiety

But if I let it go
I'm still holding on
Cause to let go fears me

Holding on gives me the ability
To finally see
That I made it bittersweet when it didn't have to
be

If I took the time to thaw my mind
And really find
The problem at hand just maybe I could finally
be

Sunflowers from Mulch

Growth is difficult
even for sunflowers in mulch
Strugglin' and strivin' to make it to the top
from the dirt
Pushin' past obstacles
But when that sunflower finally makes it
A beautiful sight to see
Just how bright that sunflower could be

Forget Me Nots

Forget Me Nots
or forget me that's okay too
whether or not you do or don't
doesn't phase me
I've been forgivin' you since you
can't forget me

Forget Me Nots
knots in my stomach
because the thought of even thinking you
you could get to me
but you couldn't

unfazed
untouched
unbothered
why bother?
I left a mark on your heart
and you left
a scar on my mental to make me remember
Forget Me Nots

Dandelion Wishes

Childhood memories
distant but they speak to me
careless journeys through and through
guided by a mother so true
tight-knit fam
loving and fun
will not settle down
until the work has been done
supportive and caring
trying and daring
always remembering the slightest
embarrassment
hold you when you cry
pick you up when you're down
yeah, sometimes they might give you a frown
but I had wishes on dandelions
of one day having my own
to hold dear to heart
until my journey is done

Thorned White Rose

Too soft to be touched
too young to be held
unable to be harmed
strong and mighty
but veiled

a spirit doused in grace
so fragrant and mild
resilience given by the thorn
each thorn a tale of the many trials

Red Tulip Whispers

Love as deep as the red hue of a red tulip so true
a grandmother's love forever runs through
she holds your dreams in her heart
and prays from the very start
the first warrior in your corner
behind the Master in the sky
a grandmother builds a mighty fortress
to help her children get by and by
she defends and she forgives
she mends and she saves lives
a grandmother's love is wondrous
it truly never dies

Magnolia Melodies

songs so sweet
lyrics healing every heart string
soothing the soul
refilling the once empty spring
melodic songs a refuge
for with their notes we find our way
to find our sacred place in hopes we never stray

Peony Promises

My grandfather was a wonderful man
I'll never let him go
He would always protect me
through rain, sleet, or snow

He would put me on the bus when I was all
ready for school
I will focus on the happy times when I'm feeling
down and blue
He taught me to always do my best and to be all
that I could be
I was his big girl now and he would always be
proud of me

I will always remembers his words because they
hold me when I cry
I will carry his love with me on this journey but
I'll always wonder why

Neon Daisy Night

In the heart of city streets
where neon lights ignite
Two spirits found each other
despite some lonely nights

Their love a portrait splattered
upon the walls so free
abstract without a picture
but yet in harmony

rhythms and beats flowing through them
a journey bound to take flight
memories being made
under the neon daisy night

Concrete Rose Resilience

Although adorned with turmoil, amidst
concrete's cold embrace
the rose defies conformity symbolizing true
grace
strength and resilience shown by her petals tales
her fragrance encompassing you in a warm
embrace
beneath the earth it grew through pavement the
hue shew
a testimony clear between the grey and drear
the concrete rose is rare delicate in embrace
her strength forever growing roots winning the
ever-long race